Am I Good E

Jude H

ISBN-13: 978-0692515129 (Sonder Ink)

ISBN-10: 0692515127

DEDICATION

To whomever I'm dating at this moment,

I'm sure I think you're just swell, darling.

ACKNOWLEDGMENTS

The process of healing is difficult and long, and I often feel like there is an imperceptibly fine line between healing and picking at wounds. These poems are dirty and dramatic; and exaggerated and overwrought; and true; and, sometimes, a desperate plea to help myself know what the current underneath is. While it can be so much easier to tell others that their words are not sewn into me, I appreciate all of the support. This entire work is a large hug, and a "thank you" to so many people. And sometimes an, "I'm sorry."

You are so much stronger than you give yourself credit for.

6th Grade Love

A sixth grade boy meets a sixth grade girl
and they fall in love
Not the *real* kind, but the *sixth grade* kind;
The kind that says,
"I'll hurt you, and I'll make mistakes, and I'm sorry in advance."

And they did hurt each other.
Take their first kiss.
He went in too fast, and she didn't tilt her face enough,
and for the next two weeks they bore black and blue bruises beneath their
forehead skin.
They didn't know if it was a metaphor or foreshadowing of things to come, but
it was
a hell of a first kiss.

And they did hurt each other.
Like when she hurt his ego every time she didn't give him the affirmation he
craved when she neglected to call him brilliant when he said things like, "The
worst part about the Ottoman Empire collapsing was that nobody had
anywhere to sit."

And they did hurt each other.
Like when he smiled and said, "you look good, honey" every time she wore
her favorite necklace.

And they did hurt each other.
Like when she pointed out the irony of kids in India making his TOMS shoes.
And so instead of falling for music or art or something that would never let
you down, like ice cream, she fell for a boy.

And they did hurt each other.
Like one day, when he decided he couldn't lie to her anymore and said, "I
never liked that stupid necklace... or you"
Maybe that was the biggest lie of all. Because *maybe* things would be easier
if they hated each other. Maybe if he left her back-down, belly-up getting
emotionally buried, his cowboy boots wouldn't seem so dusty.

But that was a lie.

The necklace wasn't awful,
but sixth grade was.

Orion's Belt

She said her favorite constellations was Orion
because she has beauty marks that come in threes
all over her body

You wanted so bad to investigate further
but being a gentleman
you just looked at her
and smiled

She said her favorite thing in the world
was to wake up in the morning
and curl up in the comforter because she loved the feeling
of being held

You wanted nothing more than to appease her
but you decided it would be better
if you just opened the door for her

She said she was scared about tonight
and all she wanted was for
someone to tell her everything would be fine

so you finally gave in
and you took her hand
and told her, not what you really felt,
but what she needed to hear

She thanked you, smiled
walked through the door
and down the aisle
to the man she loved.

For M,

This poem is for a girl named M

I think you're great. Really, I do. You've always been there for me, even when you weren't.

If that doesn't make sense to you, clearly, you aren't M.

Unless you are.

The best part about this poem is I know so many M's, and it can be anyone of them.

Am I talking about Mel or Molly or Melissa or Mary or Megan 1 or Megan 2 or Mom?

You don't know.

I keep it ambiguous enough so that you'll never know, but I'll still include things to prove that you're the person I'm talking about.

I like when we get coffee together. I like the conversations we have. I like talking to you.

Is that specific enough?

Maybe, I'll include something that you know, for sure, makes this poem about you.

I like talking about zombies with you.

Now is about when you start to wonder if I talk about zombies with everyone.

Maybe, this isn't about you.

Maybe, the girl's name doesn't even start with "M." Maybe it's shorthand for when I call you "Em," Emily.

Or maybe it's just the second letter of your name, Amanda.

Maybe, it's an upside-down "W," Wanda.

Maybe, it's just because it's the thirteenth letter of the alphabet, and you and I always joked about the number thirteen, Dana.

That last one was clearly a red herring though. That's far too complicated.

Seriously though, M, I miss you, and I hope you do well in life. You're great.

Also, stop being such a fucking bitch.

P.S. This is not for you, Mom.

I'm Going To Explode

Sometimes, I feel like my chest is going to explode, because I can't possibly feel anymore feelings for a single person.

I wake up, and the first thing I think about is you. I wonder how you slept. I wonder what you're doing today. I think about if I'm going to see you, and if not, I already miss you.

I think about you more times than I can count throughout the day. I wonder how you're doing. I miss you. I wish we were together. I think to myself, *whatever I'm doing, right now, would be better if you were here too.*

And, sometimes, I think to myself, "There is no way on Earth that I could possibly like someone more than I like this girl. I already feel like my chest is going to explode. I can't even contain my feelings for her. I'm at a loss of words when I'm with her. She makes me so nervous, and she's so darn beautiful."

Then, you're the last thing I think about when I go to sleep, and I realize, I feel like I like you even more today. Someone, all the little things about you that I love added up, and my feelings grew. My heart expanded just a little more today. I didn't think it was possible, but it happened. I'm falling in love more every day.

I can't wait to wake up tomorrow.

New Orleans Saga (8 Poems)

Like a good, liberal boy,
I had never been to the South.
River
I don't know what the mouth of the Mississippi River looks like
but I imagine it is missing teeth.

I fell in love with a girl from Ark-kan-sass,
and she quickly corrected me
that is was, indeed, not pronounced
"love."

When I went to New Orleans
there were so many people
the only landmark you could make out
was a single streetlight above the crowd.
The one everyone used to meet each other.
So we all just spun around it like moths
looking to mate.

And a girl took my hand
and led me though the crowd
she swam through the fog

New Orleans

I don't want to die in New Orleans.
Like a rat in the gutter of the French District.
Right between the Barely Legal Cabaret and the voodoo shop.
This place is fucking lonely.
My friend told me to find the highest roof I can get to, and overlook the city.
I don't think that's a good idea right now.

My Hotel

The people next to me sound Russian.
They came in late last night and talked a lot.
I can't tell if they're Russian or I just can't understand them behind the walls.
I pushed my ear hard against the connecting door, but it did little more than
concuss me.

The people across from me seem very happy.
Tell them to be quiet.

The Mississippi

I saw the Mississippi today.
It made me feel so small.
And dry.

The Roommates

I have been communicating with the people next door to me.
We pass papers underneath the shared door.
They seem nice.

The Mirror

I stood, naked, in front of the mirror
I circled everything I didn't like about myself with watercolors
I only circled my heart, but it ended up running everywhere

An Omen in Paints

I spent yesterday painting
I could never get the watercolors to do quite what I wanted
Ironic
I stared out the window for an hour, wondering if it was tall enough for me to
fall and not feel any pain
I got a text from a stranger asking me to go out with them to dinner
It probably saved my life
And the jumbalaya was good too
I got back and the paints were still trying to figure out what to do with
themselves

Pull Me Through The Streets

The air between moving bodies is the most stale and foul in the world
And nothing is harder than moving through a crowd
But you reached back and took my hand
in yours

and you pulled me.
You pulled me through the crowd,
underneath a wet streetlight.
You pulled me close, and it all felt symbolic
We never kissed, but I felt better in my soul

Books

Darling, you're a book to me.
Maybe that isn't the most romantic thing to call you but it's better than "muffin"
or "cupcake" or "pumpkin" or "sugar" or "honey" or "artificial food coloring
number 9".

You're a book to me because, sometimes, I feel like we're moving way too
fast.
Not because I don't like it, but because I'm worried we'll get to the end more
quickly.

I'm worried that you'll be a short-story instead of a novel. Or a new character
in the next chapter will be far more interesting than I could ever be. Every
time I turn a page and crease your spine, I'm 1/10 of 1mm closer to leaving
you on a shelf where one of us will collect dust, and that scares me.

So maybe I'll re-read the same line a hundred times because it's so damn
beautiful.
or maybe I'll re-read the same line a hundred times because it's so damn
beautiful.
or maybe, I'll re-read the same line a hundred times because you're so damn
beautiful.

And maybe I'll hang around page 57, when you first kissed outside a dusty
planetarium that wasn't even open. But you had the whole sky, and every star
you would ever need. Or maybe I'll re-read chapter 16, paragraph 2, where
you're handed a rock, because your love interest thought it would last a hell
of a lot longer than a flower. Or maybe I'll bookmark the best part of the story,
so I can always go back to your climax.

Tee-hee

Either way, if I end up flipping through your last pages, I hope there's a
sequel.

Haley

Don't forget the night you had with her.
How her hair curled all around
and she looked beautiful.

Don't forget that you saw her flaws
but you wanted nothing more
than to tell her you accept her.

And want her

Don't forget how she curled up into you
And ran her fingers across your chest
and tucked her head under your neck.

To feel safe.
And loved.

And she was both.

Don't forget how she moaned and smiled every time you kissed her.
Like it was the first time she'd ever been touched.
Like she was the first person you ever loved.
Like you just wanted her to be the last too.

Drinking Myself

I'm soaked up in me.
I drank too heavily of myself,
and didn't leave enough room for others to puddle in.
The drops of others can mix with my medium
but I'm already saturated.
And I just need help to dry out.

Not Done Yet

I haven't gotten to the part of the story where I say I'm ok.
Where I say I'm sorry.
Where I say how much I love everyone and everything.
I haven't brought myself to say it out loud
yet.
It's the hardest part of the story, the ending.
I'm getting there, but I don't want people to read anything yet.

Stupid Girl

I just want to kiss this stupid fucking girl on her stupid fucking face.
Probably, in the rain, because she will like stupid shit like that.
I want to buy this stupid girl fucking chocolates because
well, just because. She would probably like something dumb like that.
All I want is to drive my motorcycle across this stupid state, along the stupid beach,
and arrive at her stupid door, and tell this stupid girl that I need her in my stupid life.
And then pull her outside and kiss her stupid mouth in the fucking rain.
Girls like that type of thing, right?
I just want to tell her that I think she's perfect.
That she's got such a big heart, and she's so fucking smart, and every thing she does,
I've just fallen in love with.
And that she makes my chest dance.
And that I think she's so fucking great.
And that I normally never swear except when I'm nervous, and she fucking terrifies me,
because all I want to do is kiss this stupid girl's face.

Routines

When it gets dark, I go through the same routine every night.
I turn off every light in the house, and go to my collection of almost dead candles.
I light one on the floor, and I watch it burn out.
I wrap my arms around my body tight enough to squeeze the air out of me, but I can never seem to squeeze you out.
I squeeze tighter and tighter until I feel like you're with me again. Until I feel safe; like I'm at the home I never was

Rocks

I'm not searching for gold in this canyon.
I'm just looking for a rock smooth enough that I won't cut myself when I touch it.

Reya

Shining towers of marble, and faded pictures of people long gone surround you as you're given this fragile paper with a picture of a face.

On mine, a smiling little girl. She's missing teeth, and her blonde hair curls up just above her ears. She's strange looking.

Walk down a brick alley, where the only light reflects off our gold stars into rat's eyes.
I carry my card loosely in my hand,
and when pictures of POWs and prisons
and shooting squads and Stars of David
pass me on both sides, I grip a little harder.

I learn this girl has a name. Reya.
She's missing teeth, and her blonde hair curls up just above her ears. She's funny looking.

I'm staring at the little models of Berlin.
I can see *Mein Kampf* in the window, and crowds of people cheering for their figurine leader.
Part of me wants to scream at the little dolls, "Don't you know who he is?",
but all I find myself doing is clutching the picture a little harder.

I learn this girl has a family. A mother and father.
She's missing teeth, and her blonde hair curls up just above her ears. She's kinda cute.

On the wall is a map 8 people long, but 80,000 names are on it.
Krakow, Poland. The largest extermination ghetto in all of World War II.

I learn this girl has a home. Krakow.
I stared at the words, hoping they'd change, but they just stared back at me, saying, "I know what you feel. We all want things to be different."

I'm in a mass of people, and we're herded through the Auschwitz replica gates.
A person with a whip points left or right.

Fifteen people in front of me, and I don't know what was happening.

Eleven people in front of me, and a mother is separated from her child. The child cries over the hushed sounds of superficial soothing.

Eight people in front of me and I realize what the man with a whip was pointing to.
Left: children, sickly and others.
Right: able-bodies.
Left meant the gas chamber. Right meant a few more miserable months to live.

Five people ahead of me and I start to panic.
"This is stupid. It's just museum," I tell myself.
But that doesn't stop my hands from sweating.

One woman ahead of me, and the man takes a paper with a picture the woman is holding and rips it in two. And points left.

I stare at my picture. I can't let them take this.

I face the man with the whip, and he looks at me up and down. I don't even care which direction they point, but this picture is all I have.

He points left, and I breathe again.

I learn this girl has an age. Four.
She's missing teeth, and her blonde hair curls up just above her ears. She's beautiful.

A man mumbles the words "Juden" to me as I walk by.
I find myself in a large room meant for showers.
I want to cry, because this is just all too much to handle, but I held it in, because there's a little boy standing next to me. He's only four years old, and I don't want him to know what's happening. Four is far too young to know about the world.

The air is thick, and people are holding each other. Many are crying, but I just hold my picture. The boy sees the girl in my hands and asks if I know her.

I feel like I do, so I say, "Yes"

When we leave the chamber, you learn your child's fate.
Did they survive, or did they die.

And I can't bring myself to hand over the picture, because I'm too scared to find out what happens to Reya.

I'm too scared to let go of her.

I stand on my own, and choke back tears. Not just because of what I have seen, but what I'm about to see.

I find out this little girl has a fate. Unknown.
Her family disappeared the day before the Krakow ghetto was attacked.

This girl whose entire row of adult teeth hadn't grown in yet. And who had been growing her hair all her life, but it still wasn't past her ears. And who was smiling when this picture was taken despite everything. Despite everything.

and I cried.

Not because of what I saw. Not because of the pictures of people so thin you don't know if they're human or not. Not because my family had to escape Germany so they wouldn't have to wear gold stars on their arms. Not because I didn't know what happened to Reya... but because I know that somewhere in the world there is a smiling, blonde Jewish girl who is a survivor.

Onomonopia

Crash smash bang
She sang
out the tune of her childhood
"Don't worry, about a thing"

bash boom rumble
She mumbles
to herself words of encouragement.
"'cuz everything little thing..."

Shatter
Scatter
the sound of mom's favorite vase against the wall,
which means tonight, dads had too much to drink
"is gonna be alright"

Footsteps
coming up the stairs.
Slamming door
outside.

Which creature had left tonight?

creak creak
She knew the sound of her parent's feet
on the wood floor outside her door,
but which one was it

Please go away.

Knock knock
"Open the door, darling"
She couldn't tell by the voice who it was,
It was too slurred and thick with displaced anger.

Knock knock
The handle vibrates as the intruder tries to enter.
Turn towards the window, because it's the only way out.

Crash smash bang
She sang
out the tune of her childhood to cover up the sound of the window being
kicked out of it's frame.
"Don't worry, about a thing"

bash boom rumble
She mumbles
to herself words of encouragement to bring herself to cross the roof above
the grass
"'cuz everything little thing..."

Shatter
Scatter the sound of the door being kicked in, and her feet hitting dirt.
which means tonight, she's a free girl
"is gonna be alright"

Change

Like you, this poem is uninspired, at best.
And I know there are a lot of very critical poetry connoisseurs that will say,
"What a terrible way to start out a poem" and to them, I say, "... I agree," but
at least it's honest.

So instead, I'll start over and say something like:

Put down your bricks and bullets and Bibles,
'cuz all three of those are
causing more damage than they're worth.

There are cries from the street that fall on deaf ears.
Rich, but still deaf ears.
"You can't make change without breaking a bill"

Well, this revolution doesn't matter if you're left or right
or top or bottom
or who's watching young, Italian-Americans on the shores of New Jersey.

There is a revolution that needs to start
In music and art
and against the ex parte
and fuck Descarte,
because just *thinking* isn't enough to be.

You have to make a change
There has to be
heart.

And it doesn't matter if you're far left,
and you only eat grass
and you think trees should vote

or you're far right,
and you think only Protestants should vote
and you only eat... poor people

You've got to stand up for what you believe.
And some will tell you not to stand too high

for fear you'll block the person behind you's view,

but instead of throwing flaming flowers
or a molotov clematis
just politely turn around and offer them a spot
in (y)our victory march.

They'll call you crazy now
but the day after the revolution,
even the most radical is a moderate

And, yeah, this poem
doesn't show much more emotion
than a half-built teddy bear
in a child's arms,
before she sews a heart into its sleeve,
and believes that it can change her whole world.

This isn't much more
than a pretty scene
of fallen leaves
on ground water, sheen
Telling you that it looks good now
but in between
the bad and the worse,
it might get better.

It gets better.
It gets better.
It gets better.
If you make it.

Forgive Me

Forgive me for not answering
For not picking up the phone when you called
For not coming to the door when you rang
For not listening when you talked.
Forgive me for not answering
Maybe a wake is not the place for forgiveness

[Hint]

She was a [adjective] [noun]
One with [adjective describing her personality].
He was a [opposing adjective] [noun].
Never the less, they loved each other.
Even up until [subtle hint at major accident]

Beginning End

Beginning

We don't talk much

I walk through the door to your place

We kiss

We make love

It's over

Ending

It's over

We make love

We kiss

I walk through the door to your place

We don't talk much

Lifeguarding

I want to become a lifeguard
so that I can save people
so that I can save myself.

To pull them out of the churning sea
and fight against the currents
and my demons.

To scrape my bones against the coral
and swallow a sea's worth of salt
to drag this person onto gritty sand
and finally feel like I'm out of harms way.

To breath into them
and fill them up with everything I've ever wanted in life.
To pressurize their lungs with memories of their childhood
and inspiration
and art,
until they cough up hope
and spit love back into my mouth.

To watch the family they didn't know loved them
squeeze the air back out of them
and tell them that things will be ok.
That things will be different now.
That when they thought they lost them
they saw all the things they've ever done wrong
and they swore to change.
So they hold them
and me.

I want to save a life
and I just want it to be my own.

Wrunk Driting

i want to wiutke drunk.
i think oill be more in touch with eveythin i feel
if only i can get past all of the thigns i feel.

Too many metaphrs and a despaarte need to sound poetic.
just write the truth.

im not ok.

Just rwte the truth over and over until your nails pop off
and you cna use them as tiny sailboats in a tiny painting
that you;ll never paint
because you dont know how to paint
and youre drunk.
im not ok imnotok im not ok.
My nails have yert to fall off, but im sounding repetative.

I can hear my voice hwn i type.
Id rather hear yours.

Impossible Things

I don't want to write of impossible things
like falling in love
or legible prescriptions

People Who Say You Only Fall in Love Once Are Liars.

People who say you only fall in love once are liars.

They say that a good love will only happen once in your life, so make it count, and hold on tight to its hand, and don't miss out, or fuck it up.

But that's the thing about love. You don't need to worry about breaking it, because there's always another.

I fell in love for the first time when I was five years old. I heard "Don't Let Me Down," and I fell hard. And so did the CD.

That was the first of many scrapes.

I fell in love again in third grade.

I was listening to The Who. Somewhere between "Pinball Wizard" and "I'm Free," I knew that I was going to grow my hair out, and spend the rest of my life with this album.

It wasn't an easy road, and it finally ended on my thirteenth birthday. That was when a friend of mine bought me every album The Used ever recorded.

I used the back of a skateboard to sand down the knees of my pants, so I felt like I had the right to listen.
I took a safety pin and begged it to go through my lip.
I did all the unhealthy things you do to change yourself so that you can fit better into the spaces of what you love.

But the eyeliner soaked into my retinas, and I got sick of the taste of black nail polish,
so I needed to move on. I threw my fingerless gloves into the ocean.

After many years, and many times falling in love, and falling, and falling in love, and falling, I sit and listen to the sounds of an acoustic guitar sing its death rattles.
And I think it's perfect.

The people that say love doesn't happen more than once are wrong.
They've never heard a guitar cry.

Or a harmonica heart.

Or been in that brutally possible love.

The kind of love where it won't ever happen again... every time.

People who say you only fall in love once are deaf to the world around them.

Amnesia After the Accident

The way you described it was like
a comet hitting the atmosphere.
My motorcycle bursting like a star
across the freeway.

You said that I never saw the car coming,
but even if I did
I would have been too stubborn to stop.

I ask you who I am
and you tell me.
I ask you who you are
and you explain.
I ask you who we are
and you stop.

They say when the bomb
dropped on Hiroshima
Silhouettes were permanently burned
onto the sides of buildings,
because when there is that much pain
ghosts will always be trapped in the walls.

Ghosts will always be trapped in these walls now.

You told me about the shattered door framed
and how history repeated itself
when it exploded out the capillaries
on your arms
and the first time I blackened your eye.

The same eyes that are staring at me
that show the type of pain that says
"I want to come back,
but we both know how that will go"
The kind of pain that screams
many things
but lets "Why" hang in the air
because there is never a good enough answer for that.

You are the first person
I have ever met.
But after you leave,
I will do what I can
to make you my last.
I do not know myself,
but I hate me.

I never want there to be another you
and I just want to free these ghosts.

Cheek Kiss

I kissed a girl on her cheek!
Yes, you heard me right. That wasn't a typo of the mouth. I said, "I kissed a girl on her cheek".

Who does that?

This isn't <u>The Notebook</u>. Maybe if it had been raining, and I'd driven away on a motorcycle, it would have been more acceptable, but let's be honest, it still wouldn't have been a forehead kiss.

A forehead kiss says "I love you for more than just the way your skin feels on mine.
Or that you never wear heels.
Or that I get shivers when you sing.
Or that you only listen to records.
Or that you like to read my palms everyday, just so we have an excuse to hold hands.
Or that you point out the irony of kids in India making my TOMS.
Or that when I said I liked History in school, you said your favorite class was the proletariat.
Or that sometimes, when you smile, I feel like I'm having a heart attack, and then I realize my heart isn't dying, it's just dancing."

A forehead kiss says that "I love you for everything about you".

But I didn't give that kiss. No, I gave a kiss with no hint of romance
One you'd give to a stranger in France.
Or a partner in dance.
Or I'm pretty sure JT gave to Lance.
Or someone at a family reunion.

And if you're uncomfortable hearing that, think about how I felt.

The girl that I had a crush on for four years
and it took half that time
and seven beers
just to get up the courage to ask her
"Hello?"
As if she was supposed to know that was an invitation to coffee.

When really all I wanted to say was, "I like you. For your skin and your shoes, and your songs and your slight sideways smiles, and the way you make me feel like I'm dying."

So why don't we just put our hands together even if our love lines don't match.
In fact, the only match we'll have is the one I'll carry around for you in my back pocket for those nights you complain it's a little too cold.

Because I don't want to carry around an extra jacket for you.
It's not because I don't love you or because I'm lazy.
It's just that... ok... I'm a little lazy.

But, honestly, my arms should be enough to keep you warm.

Listen, I've seen you at your best, and I've seen you at your... sweatpants and ice cream nights, and I just want to take *both*.

That's what I was trying to say, and I get that a cheek kiss didn't really relay that message, so maybe next time, I'll go for something more serious, like an eskimo kiss.

The Bridge

I went to a bridge
and stared off the side

and I wish I could say I saw something of worth
but all I saw was my reflection at the bottom.

I didn't jump,
but I did figure out that I didn't want to die
like this.

Not at the worst point in my life.
I'd rather die right when my life hits the peak
'cuz it'll only get worse from there.

No, I didn't want to die after you left me
but I did want to take a bullet after we first kissed

The first night we slept together
we didn't touch each other.

There was a pocket of air between us
but I was too scared to get rid of it.
But I could have opened my wrists up to you that night.

When we went down to the lake
and finished each other's paintings,
I could have searched for rope the entire drive home.

So, when I went to the bridge
and stared at myself,
I found out something important.

I found out there was a lot of good in this world.
And maybe I don't have any in my hands
but I can find it
and maybe I can go to the bridge soon

I Fell in Love With an Actress

I fell in love with an actress
She came on during the first act
and looked at me
and smiled
and winked.

The words she said
she said to me.

By the time she had to leave
I didn't want an intermission.

She said we needed it
and it was for the best.

When she came back for the second act,
the music crescendoed
and it all felt like too much
but it was good.

Every line she said
reverberated in my rib cage
and the way the light sparkled off her eyes
blinded me.

It wasn't until the curtains dropped
that I realized what it was.

She had said her lines
and moved to all her marks
and looked beautiful

I had fallen in love with an actress
and she had done her job
and acted.

Coworker 1

I fell in love with a coworker.
I want to rip the sky
open and tell her
that she can do better.

I want to hold her
when her man isn't
and man
but a worm
that burrows and hides
and makes her fingers bleed
while she claws at the dirt
to find him

I want to get drunk
and mumble screams
into a phone
only so I'll have an excuse
to tell her how goddamn beautiful she is.
Only so I can say it was alcohol
and a wrong number
the next morning.

I want to burn the moon
into my skin
to that I can glow
enough to make her life with someone bad
a little brighter
just by standing next to her.

I fell in love with a coworker
and all I want is to write to her.
To whisper notes,
scrawled by the nervous hand
of a kindergartner
in his favorite colored crayon,
right into her chest,
so that it can skip the ears
and brain

and go straight to the heart.
I want to make her world explode
with words she's never heard,
and rhythm she's never felt,
and tunes she'll never sing
with anyone but me.
But the curse of a poet is that you can never
find the words that you've spent years writing
when it comes time to say them face to face.

The Child of an Alcoholic

The child of an alcoholic
sits alone in the bathtub
cutting through his fragile exterior
to see if he really is filled with
red wine

His father
a brave bull
and his mother
a white Russian
will never understand how the smell of
tequila spit
stays in your hair
and your clothes

But this boy is a stinger
a locust
a rusty nail

and no one will serve him anything
but skin

His eyes filled with champagne
sparkled and fizzed
The child of an alcoholic
sits alone in the bathtub

Grandfather

My grandfather was a cantankerous man.
I was five when I spilled oil on his carpet.
And he was... old when he screamed at me.

My entire life, that is how I pictured him;
wrinkled and hunched over
like a Navy bomb
exploding at me.

I was 23 when I learned that his last words
were my own name.
My grandfather hid his heart,
but he cared more about me than I ever knew.

Goodbye, Grandfather

I don't remember the room
or the couch
or what the curtains looked like

All I remember is your eyes
and how it's the only time in my life
I've ever seen them filled up
to the brim
with liquid
I didn't know you possessed.

Your father was gone.
You didn't use the word, "dead"
until I asked why.

The crinkles around your eyes gave you away
when your eyelids trembled briefly
before giving up.

I cried when you did
because I had never seen my dad
be anything other than
a rock.

I don't remember the GI Joes
or what was said
or how it ended

Just your eyes
wrinkled and swollen and wet
from a lifetime of holding this in.
From all the things I'm sure you wanted to say
but you didn't.

From the same things I hold in
because in this family
we're rocks.

And all that will be remembered is our eyes

Regretted Last Words

A father buries his son.
The last words he spoke
are stuck burning the back of his throat.
"You are not good enough."

The Note You Left on the Window of Your Car in the Garage With the Engine Running
I'm sorry
I wasn't good enough

The Surgeon to the Parent
I'm sorry
I wasn't good enough

Left Under Your Wedding Ring
I'm sorry
I wasn't good enough

A Boy At His Father's Death Bed
I'm sorry
I wasn't good enough

A Father on His Death Bed to His Boy
I'm sorry
I wasn't good enough

A Letter to My Editor
I'm sorry
I wasn't good enough

Stream of Consciousness on a First Date

This will go well.
I think.
Maybe not.
Make eye contact.
Be normal.
Nod.
Smile.

Does sitting like this make me seem open?
I should uncross my arms.
There's a stain on my shirt.
I should have worn black.
Nod.
Or something that doesn't show stains
and wrinkles
and sweat
weight gain
how nervous I am.

Do I look in her eyes?
Both eyes?
Back and forth?
Nod.
Just one eye.
The right one.
Why the right?
Switch to the left.
Symmetry: back to the right.
Now you're just switching back and forth.
It's what you were trying to avoid in the first place.
Right between the eyes.
Nose.
Mouth.
Lips.
Blowjob.
Stop.
Listen.
Nod.
What is she talking about?

Who the fuck is Craig?
Stop staring.

Glance down at my tea.
Pick it up and swirl the liquid around.
Don't drink.
Just swirl.
Nod.
Nod.
Nod.
Nod off.
Nod.

Smile.
With your eyes.
Too much.
Less.
Not enough.
Stop changing your smile.

"What do you think about it?"

Stop.
Nod.
Look down.
Swirl.
Smile.

"I think it's great."

Stephanie

We spent seven hours
staring at the stars
with our backs against concrete.

You told me about every one of you flaws
and I showed you all of my cracks.
We were both so scared,
so I whispered,
"If this is the worst that can happen from being human,
things will be ok."

There were times I saw black holes in your eyes
begging to be filled with someone else.

But I am just a meteor
praying to find someone's gravity.

We stared at the stars,
but they were vast and terrifying.
It felt like staring at ourselves.
And all of our worries.
And everything in life that scared us so much
seemed to come at once.
And we were forced to recognize why we were trembling.

We saw ourselves in the light of the dark
and shared what it meant to be fatally human.

And you whispered,
"If this is the worst that can happen from being human,
things will be ok."

Spoken Word Sex

A girl masturbated
to my poetry last night.

She had me read
and read
and read
until we both crescendoed at the same time.

My words were wet and dripping.
Her eyes were soaking it all up.
We were both lost in each other.

Music Festival Sexual Assault

He was on top of you
heavy, like a fog.
Your friends were not surrounded by it yet
and he tried to pull you away.
You motioned for your friends to join you
so that you wouldn't be lost at sea.

All night, he pulled
and prodded
and pleaded
for you to go with him.

You were both high on everything.
Mostly each other.

But you still said, "no"

When he pulled you, and both fell to the ground,
I came over to help.

I tried to tell you what he was doing
what you could do
that he was a strong tide you didn't need to swim in.

You pushed me away
and disappeared into the crowd.
I lost you.

A man at a university tells kids all the time
that he once "lost a student."
He lost him to suicide,
and you can see it in his eyes
in his bones.

But everyone feels like they lost that boy.
There was always something they could have done to save him.
If only they picked up the phone
if only they were nicer
if only they did that one magical thing

he wouldn't be lost.

But he didn't lose that boy,
and I have to keep telling myself I didn't lose this girl.

Sleeping Hands
My hand woke up on top of yours this morning
Yours was fast asleep, but mine got a little restless
And things seemed like they were getting a little serious
and mine got nervous

It put on some thimbles and slowly
walked down your stomach.
It paused at that crease in your hip to turn around
and admire the situation it found itself in

It tipfingered its way back to my shoulder
Where it curled up into a ball
The position it was used to

But you groaned
and I felt your hand walking up and down me
trying to find its partner

When the tip of your middle finger finally found my hand
folded and hunched up next to my neck,
it didn't force it out
It just waited patiently

With a soft pressure to remind my hand to keep breathing

And then our fingers walked back down to our sides
with our thumbs intertwined
and went back to sleep

Coffin

I spent my whole life trying to break out of a box
that I kept myself in.

Please, do not bury me in a box

Bury me on a plank of redwood
so I can soak back into the Earth

Let the water weep into my bones
and let the sky warm the dirt on my skin

I don't want to live in a box
and I certainly don't want to die in one.

Sound Waves

You
You are
You are a
You are a sound
You are a sound wave
That takes my ear drums and
smashes them against ocean rocks
every time I try to listen to a
sweet melody, I end up in
so much pain because
you are just a sound wave, and like
a sound wave, you come and
you go, and I never seem
to know when you peak
and when you
might
stop

Falling

A sky

A light

                       A boy in blue

There are yellow leaves   Who could stop the world

       Just about everywhere   With nothing more than a toy gun

       But the grass is still a bit wet   And a smile. So, he walked

            And the fog is a bit dense without looking

                And a car that doesn't see anything in blue

                And the world and the gun fall apart

                And a smile stops
                faster than
                   brakes do.
                        And there is a sky
                  And a light
                     And yellow

          And red

                       and blue.

                And there are leaves
       just about

everywhere.

Hanging

They say that we are put on this Earth
to learn how to be good.
And when you learn that
you can go back to whatever God created you.

Or at least that's what I've told myself
ever since we found the boy lying in his closet.
I say "boy" because it's easier than saying "brother"
and I say "laying" because it's not as hard as saying "hanging"
Or "suicide"

I can't stop thinking about hanging myself.
What a terrible way to die.
I already tried it,
and I only hurt my head
and broke the wall.

Hanging.
Hanging.
Hang ing.
Ha ng i ng.
It sounds like what it is.
A moment when you're waiting for it to be over.

Just waiting.
And waiting.
And wa it i ng.

to swing each side
or close your eyes
or or stop struggling.
Just hanging around
waiting for something to change.

And I want this poem to stretch out
further than you wanted it to.
I don't want this to end.
I want you to be uncomfortable.
I want every word to stretch on way too long

long enough that you don't quite know if it will end
Almost as if every word is
hanging

A Found Note

A note you drew
slipped into a book
I swore I would someday read.

It's been years since I've thought of it
or you.

But this note sent me back
and the weight of the void between us
smothered me.

"I'll always be there for you."

A Bullet and a Dagger

Life is fast
and the transition is quick.

That's the crazy part about it.

You're here
and then you're not.

You just cease.

No more.

Boom.
Snap.
Off like the bride's pajamas.

And God forbid you know you're going.
Then, it's painful.

So, you're stuck.
You're stuck in this in-between
this haunting limbo
a bullet or a dagger.

We need not be scared of either,
for all of us will go.

Teaching

I want to teach
so I can show kids
that it is ok
to not be ok.

I want to show them
that
we are all broken.
And that it's human,
and being human is ok
It's beautiful.

I want to tell them
about dinosaurs
and Oxford commas
and the way the planets spin,
and how everything relates back to love.
Not for each other
but for life
and not just life
but living.

I want to teach
in a way where
it is ok to say that I don't know the answer
if you ask me,
but God dammit if I don't have one next time you ask.
Where, in a room of 400,
the students in the back
feel like I know their eye color
and I will call everyone
"Miss First Name"
or "Mister Last Name"
so everyone knows,
in their bones,
that they are worthy

And everything they will do in life
is worthy.

And one day,
maybe when they are broken,
and do not have answers
to the questions that kids ask,
they can roll their sleeves up
to a room of 400
and show everyone how fragile they are.

A Recording Of Your Voice

I
I love
I love you
You
stutter
every
word
because
it never
seems to come out right the
first time you say it. That's ok, my
darling. That's ok. It's never easy to be
vulnerable. But that's why we practice it so
much. Every time we breathe in and out
to the sound of music,
and when we chant along to
the steady flow of
the blood in our arms when we roll
up our sleeves and show the world,
the entire world,
all two of us,
that it is ok to
stutter
and say the words over and over
again, until everyone is aching
from the sound of,
"I love you"

The Common Thread

Everyone in our family
has died of cancer.
It is the common thread
that unites us all.
So, when my father told me
that he had it too
we didn't know what to say;
at least out loud.
We said so much with our eyes,
and we made jokes
about doctors
and how we all die.
We all die.
When you lose everyone
to the same thing,
and you live in fear
your entire life
of having that same disease
your whole life revolves
around that fear
that aching
that tense-feeling
your muscles get
when the word comes up.
What do you do
when you have it now to?

Ten Hours of Applause

I am an empty vessel
at best.
A boy trying to be a man
trying to be a boy
trying to be a man
trying to be something
worthy.

I have people that praise me
for all the things they say I do,
and letters and emails and phone calls
from people who tell me how much
they love me.
And how they've never met someone like me.
And awards to commemorate
crowning achievements.
How have I tricked everyone
into thinking I deserve any of it?

Maybe, I do.
Maybe I do.
But I know that
none of it helps
when I feel alone.
An entire room of people
for me.
And a tailored suit
and a shiny paper
in a cherry wood frame.
Good for me.
It's self-masturbatory.
And I can never understand how so many
God damn people
can think of me
so differently
than I think of myself.

So, smile
and nod,

and thank them all
and be humble.
It's easy to be humble
when you don't believe what they say.

And when you decide
to tell a person
that you're not ok,
they ask why.
"Why not, when all of us love you?"
"What's wrong when everything is so great?"
"Why do you feel like you aren't doing enough, when you're doing
everything?"
People don't get it.
But, I guess, I don't expect them to
because I don't either.
It's like a round of applause
ten hours long
and I don't know what we're clapping for,
and I'm the only one standing up saying,
"Why are we clapping? This isn't a real thing."
And everyone laughs and keeps clapping.
It's all so empty.

A Creation

I created this story
like I created my life.
And I wish that
I had control over either one of them

Words like IV's

I stopped writing once you got cancer.
There just weren't words that were honest anymore.
We always used our words like swords and shields
but what good is a shield if it's made of glass?

The ink well
your bones
ran dry.

My page
your skin
sickeningly white.

Both faces
empty

You can't fill a chair with vowels
or pentameter
or letters you wish you'd written.

There just aren't words
that can fill the air
in a way that makes things different
or bridges gaps in communication
that have formed over lifetimes.

So, we just sit in silence
and let the words we never said hang
and drip
one by one
straight into our blood
hoping they'll save us.

A Rainy Goodbye

Few things hurt as much
as the stabbing
inside your lungs
from a sharp inhale
of cold air.

Wet overcast
and fitted black suits
with thin ties
to suffocate us.
To keep us from speaking.

Everything is wet
and cold
and painful.
Even the bits of dirt under my nails
from the handful I threw into your hole.
What a strange tradition.
As if a handful could cover up a life.

When a Girl Asked What That Black X Underneath My Skin Was

When I was young
I took my father's Boyscout pocketknife
and I traced the veins in my arms.
Up and down
like highways
carrying bits of me
to anyone who would have it.

I sat in a dry bathtub
going back and forth
with the dullest part of the blade.
It rubbed more than anything.

With every pass
I thought about a friend
who would never miss me.
There's something about people
continuing on with their lives
that invokes a special kind of fear.
There's no reason they should cease to function,
but a child wants to think
that everyone revolves around them.

Some people close their eyes when they make a final decision.
I didn't know how to blink
when I finally pushed the blade into my arm.
There wasn't as much cutting
as just pushing.
Just a force trying to get inside me.
Farther than anyone else cared to be.

To this day,
I can feel where the few stitches that never came out are.
Small lines under a scar
to remind me that
I may never heal.
And that the real pain
is what others feel
when we all have to rebuild.

A Baseball Cap Too

A shoe in the road
a ball in the gutter
a drunk behind bars
don't make a mother feel better

Blood Clot of Soliloquies

Tip
Trip
Drip
Drop
Rain on a roof
A drunk on a floor
with a typewriter
on his head
and on his
nail beds
But a blood clot
of soliloquies
is having trouble passing

Islands and Mainland Fires

There's a feeling
that does't have words.
The urge to run
when everything
is going well.
The urge to leave
while they're still
curled up into you.
The urge to destroy
the one good thing you've found.

There are no words
to express the helplessness
and loss you feel
once you've been found.

It's the ache a sailor feels
being at sea
when all he loves is water.

There is so much pain
in not being able to help
feeling like you will never be content
when everything is what you've wanted.

This person is good
and they make you better
but you want to make
a fire
on a bridge
to burn down
your return to the mainland
after you've spent a life
escaping an island.

If You Were a Fish

If you were a fish,
I'd learn how to swim.
If you were a bird,
I'd fly on a whim.
'cuz maybe you ain't
what others want you to be.
But whatever you are,
you're perfect for me.

Hippoplatyparoo

A hippo, a platypus, a kangaroo too
All came together like you'd never knew
They stood on one's shoulders with trench coat and hat
The head was quite little, the bottom was fat.
They acted like one beast, a hippoplatyparoo.

They thought it quite funny they made something new
Like crazy 'ol animals out of Peru.
But all of their friends knew this wasn't true
on top of the hippo, the platypus sat
on the shoulder of him, the roo and the hat.
Waddling 'round making noise like kazoo
The new, funny beast- hippoplatyparoo.

A Circle of Light

Pitch
Coal
Smog
and other things to describe
the blackness of this room.

Desert
Stabbing
Leaking
adjectives and nouns to let you know how my eyes feel
after spending a night staring at the space underneath my door.

The only light here comes form the half inch underneath the portal.
It sprays onto the floor just enough
let me see silhouettes
of monsters.

Thump
Beat
Freeze
and words to describe my heart
when in the deadest part of the night
that light was eclipsed.

A Poet and a Mortician

A poet and a mortician
drink together.
Both overwhelmed
by the weight of a human heart.
And by how many things
they have buried this week.

The Motorcycle Trip Saga (14 Poems)

Sail

My backpack is a sail
A folded piece of cloth
that extends to eat air
and pull me back
at the most inopportune times.
As soon as I am getting close
I sail away.
Today, I am on the back
of a motorcycle
with my backpack
sailing across the state

Dani

A bartender told me a place to camp
and said if it didn't work out
to return to the bar.
I drove in circles for 45 minute
in a parking lot
so I could walk back in & see her again

American River

There is nothing more American than the American River
Running straight through the heart of Folsom
A city famous for its prison
and a song by Johnny Cash
A river that can't live up to its own reputation
A trickling stream on both sides
of an unnecessary dam.
A monolith to remember what
we pretend was once there
or so the legend goes
A river that smells like
prostituted needles
and homeless fish
left to die

Forgotten
What an American river.

Jamba Juice

I got a blowjob from a stripper
for a $2 giftcard
to Jamba Juice
that I said had $75 on it.
Clearly, there are things I'm not proud of

Gumbalala

I asked a gas station attendant
where the next major city was.

She laughed and said,
What do you consider major? Gumbalala.

Gumbalala?
I asked

She shook her head.
No. Gumbalala.

I'm sorry. Was that Gumbalala?

No. Gumbalala.

I don't think I'm hearing your correctly.

Gumbalalala.

Every time you say it, it gets longer.

No. It's always Gumbaleela.

That wasn't at all the same

Gumbaleeloola

Now, you're not even trying
I just want a city with
traffic lights
and a population of more
than just the people passing through it

Fort Bragg

For 146 miles
it served as a beacon
of hope.
It was so cold outside
when I finally stopped
I forgot that I had been
shaking for 3 hours.

98 miles
my hands are numb

56 miles
I can't move anything
yet all my muscles
are doing tap dances

40 miles
I just want warm water.

31 mile
I'd be happy with just a warm cup
something to push against my chest.

16 miles
my nail beds are dark purple
with white rings
like smiling half devils

4 miles
I have nothing left in me

Fort Bragg
Just as run-down as every other city

It has nothing more to offer
than a bar
with a CLOSED sign
and another out-of-business hotel.
182 miles to Eureka

Fully-catered Reindeer Party

I saw some deer today.
They looked like reindeer.
There was a whole group of them.
Like they were having a party.
A reindeer party.
What do reindeer do for a party?
I'll bet they eat food.
But it's winter, so there isn't much to eat.
So they're forced to eat each other.
Until there is only one reindeer left.
My money would be that Donner would survive.
Nothing sounds more fun than
a Donner party.

Folsom

A city that hasn't grown up yet
and is living off Johnny Cash's coattails

Good people
and good toilet paper though

Space Blanket

I've been hearing Vince's laugh
all week.
Not during any times in particular-
Just when I hear it.
I think my brain knows
when I need to hear it most.
That thunder that comes from his lungs
and explodes against my ears
and I can't think of anything else.

It's a blanket
from the cold
and shakes
and a wet body.
I used an emergency hand warmer tonight.
I placed it on the back of my neck
and I thought of Caitlyn.
Her hands rubbing out the knots
in my shoulders.
I closed my eyes
and rocked my body
to the tune of her hands
wincing when she pushed too hard.
Rocking back & forth
in soaked clothes
in a tent
blowing in a rain storm.
Every part of me numb
except where her hands create something
I close my eyes
and hear Vince's laugh.

Silverlake

I woke up in a Silverlake studio.
Not the good part.
I don't want you to think I got money.
It smelled like sour alligator whiskey
and fabric softener.
The cheap kind.
I woke up on a couch
in a Silverlake studio.
A couch the girl told me
a pornstar put his penis on
two days earlier.
She put a cover down for me though.
It was a little damp.
Like gasoline.
Not supreme.
Regular.
I woke up on a covered couch

in a Silverlake studio
with a friend in her bed
10 feet away
all night.
I thought about sending her a letter
maybe a postcard
to let her know I missed her
and wanted to be in the same bed
but postage is just too expensive
and I was only 10 feet way
in a Silverlake studio.

Torture

Every writer wants to be tortured
so they can write about it
and sound meaningful.
And write and talk about
how much they just want
to be well.
So they drink and dope
and torture themselves
so they can stay writers.
The worst thing that can happen
to a writer
is realizing
they aren't as tortured
as they think.

Hands

I woke up with my hands
feeling like they weren't there
Just bags of numbness.
I laid on the floor
face down
with my ams crossed
underneath me.
My blood couldn't leave
my heart.
So, I couldn't feel anything.

I moved my arms
and the blood came back
and it felt like I was
getting stabbed all night.

Big Sur

I went to a cabin in Big Sur
like Kerouac
and so many before me did.
To get away from myself.
To find myself.
To heal.
There's so much torture
and ache
in these bones.
So, I went to a cabin
the same cabin.
I laid on the same floor.
Wrote on the same desk.
Held my face
in my hands
and soaked in the same river
that everyone else did.
It was supposed to help me heal.
But all I found
were the same feelings,
but now I was in Big Sur with them.

The Most Personal Poem

This is a poem
just for you.
No one else.
Don't share it.
Cut it out
and sew it
to the inside of your sleeve
So it sits against your veins.
No one can see it
but you.
Because beautiful things
don't need to ask
to be looked at.
This a a quiet poem
you whisper to yourself
so you know you are loved.
Carry it like the world.

French Toast Morning

I woke up
to your back
and the smell
and sizzle
of french toast.

And I was in a blanket
on the couch
facing the kitchen
and the girl
cooking in her underwear and a shirt.

I stared at the curves of your butt
underneath your cloth
while you asked,
"Do you like jam?"

I can count on one hand
how many people
have cooked breakfast for me.
You are the only girl
who has slept over
and stayed in the morning
to cook for me
Smiling in your underwear.

I don't know why you're so good to me.
I'm going to marry you when you're done.

Trees

When my child cries
I will hold up a mirror
to show him the tiny trees
that are in the grooves & mountains
of his irises.
It's hard to cry when you see
that much beauty.

When he cries,
I will tell him about bullies
and how they are only
picking on him
because they're scared
that no one will ever see
their trees.

It has nothing to do
with the fact that he
said he wanted to be a princess when he grows up.
Because, honestly, who wouldn't want to be royalty?

When he burrows his head into a pillow
surrounded by LEGOs
and a dog
and a father
mumbling phrases that
sound like, "why?"
I will tell him about
people.

And how we're all
put on this Earth
to find others,
and then fit them
into our lives.

We're all here
to open gardens
in our chest

and share the trees
in our eyes.

It's ok to cry.
Your tree needs water every now and then.
But I will make sure to tell him that there is so much sun
in his life.
Don't let others cloud it out.

When my child cries,
I will hold up a mirror
to show him the tiny trees
that root themselves
around the corners of each iris.

We will sit in silence
until we can sit and cry
and laugh
about the world
and all of the people
that want to push us over
or all the tall things
in the world
we can fall off of
or rough streets
we scrape our knees on.
But we can get up
with gravel in our palms
and show the world
our trees

Build A Nest

I don't want you to help
because you cannot.
Please, don't give me books about
"8 Easy Steps To Cure Depression"
or links to articles about
a Suburbanite who left everything
to explore the world
and now he's cured.
Good for him.

Life is not a bookstore.
You cannot browse the options
before picking your favorite.
If things were that easy
we'd all be in the self-help aisle
reading our penises longer
and our parents more living
and using every get rich quick scheme
that exists
just to buy a house
with an elevator
to the garage
just to abandon it all
and cure ourselves.
Then, our friends could send articles
about us.

Please, do not try to help me.
Build me a nest
and lay with me in it.
We may be there for days
or lifetimes
but I don't know how to help you
help me.
So, just build me a nest
and lay with me in it.

A Death Too Young

I'm worried I'm going to die.
It's a recurring theme in my writing.
Death
Love
Sex
Regret.
Perhaps, they're all so similar
it's hard to separate them out.

I'm nervous I'm going to die
on a motorcycle
on a trip
in the middle of Yosemite
in the rain
on a Saturday night
because no drivers ever look both ways on Saturday.
God forgives on Sundays anyways.

I'm scared I'm going to die
without having said anything
to anyone
that had meaning.

My grandfather died in a hospital bed
whispering my name into the air.
That's the most intimate thing he ever said to my father.

I'm never going to get to tell my sister how proud I am
or my mother how loving I am
or my father how sorry I am.

Sorry for not trying harder
and accepting him
in all his tarnished glory.

He is faded bronze
and I kept wanting him to be gold.

There are things that need to be said

over and over
until we can only breathe those words

"It's ok. We are ok."

I am going to die before I say them, but everyone should know them.

Sonder

A break to tie your shoes
A conversation on the playground
A kiss on her cheek
A bandaid for you knee
A 12-grade writing assignment
A traffic light
A day listening to vinyl records
An afternoon shopping at thrift stores
A late-night date, overlooking the water
A kiss on your forehead
A kiss on her cheek
A night of fresh baked cupcakes
A motorcycle ride
A moment of sonder
An entire life
All of it leading up to a singular moment.
That you don't control.
But every action in your life
pushes you off the edge of a cliff.
A moment.
A collection.
A culmination of your life.
In a moment.

Alarm Clock

I give you this watch
for you to wear.
It has an alarm set to
8:00 pm
every night.

I have a matching watch
that I will wear,
so that I don't feel alone.

I want you to wear it
so I know that
no matter where I am
I am connected to someone.
I won't be alone.

I left on my trip with a bag
and my watch.
You stayed back with a book
and your watch.

I never made it back.
But your watch still rings
at 8:00 pm
every night.
You aren't alone.

uamee

"What are you looking for"
she asked.
A menu down.
"Octopus."
"No"
she says.
"I mean, like in general."
"Sushi?"
He seems unsure.
"Like, you and me."
"I've never though about that."
He picks the menu back up
as he searches for uamee.

Dear Mom

Dear Mom,
I'm sorry I didn't write
yesterday,
I was busy.
I'll always love you.

Dear mom,
I saw something today
I can't put into words.

Dear mom,
I'm still alive
but, sometimes,
I wish I weren't.

Dear mom,
I don't know if I can do this
anymore.
You told me the army
wasn't for me.
Dying isn't for anyone, mom.

Dear mom,
I'm scared.
There's talk that there'll be a firefight soon.
and I keep thinking about
what I saw.
I'm sorry I keep writing about it.
It's just been really tough forgetting.
Don't worry. I'll be ok.

Dear mom,
Tomorrow, we'll be leaving.
Some combat orders
to ambush a convoy.
Who knows?
They don't tell us much.
I just don't want to end up being
what some other person

writes to his mother about.
I'll write soon.
I love you.

Dear Mrs. Hoffman,
We regret to inform you...

A Park at Night

A blanket soaks up the grass
in exactly the way we begged it not to.
And I soaked her up
exactly how she begged me to.

Hair in mouths
and grass on palms
and scratches on backs
and stars reflecting off
a thousand points
on the backs of my knees
and undersides of elbows
and where sweat collects.

There are no cars driving by
this late at night.
Which means it's just her
and I.
And the muttered sound of
"Don't get me sick"
before we began.

Under a Piano

You played piano brutally beautifully
and I laid under the musical beast
so that you could surround me

Every note from the middle C down
shook my heart cage
And all the A's and D's and G^{add9}'s
danced against my eardrum
slowly clicking their heels
against my nerves

It was a happy song
but you played it in a way
that made me die

over and over and $\cdot \|$

Your flats reflect off the wood floor
and from where I am,
I can almost see up your dress
But I can't move because
the vibrato is in my bones

I don't typically stay up late,
but watching the sun
finally pour across the floor
while I hid under your life
that made me die again.

An Introduction

I met a girl whose first words to me were
  I had anodder dog
  but he died.
She put her palms up
as if she was carrying the world.
Quite the introduction

I had pictured this moment for months
thinking I would shake her hand,
but she had just finger painted her cereal.

I asked her what she did today,
and between bites of cherry tomatoes
the color of her cheeks,
she told me about cooking and gardening.
  Lots of things to do
  for a four year old
I said
  I ohmos five.
  In nine mumfs.
Cherry tomato.
  One, two, fwee, four, five
Cherry tomato.
  six, sefen, eight, nine.
  Nine mumfs. Pretty soon.
Cheery tomato.

I nodded.
She had a tattoo of a pony on her arm
and a secret in her eyes.
  I have a picture of a
  pwincess in my rwoom.
  I show you.
She climbed off the chair
much taller than she
and scooted to her room
disappearing behind the wall.
Her head poked back out
with a single hand

101

waving me off my seat.
            Come ear!
            I ave to show you!

Her mom and I walked to her room
as this little human
show me her most valued treasure
and this mother human
showed me her most valued treasure
as I took in
all this treasure.

For Madeline

Your eyes look like rain
on a frozen lake
There is no sadness in there
They look fresh
like a iceberg
like they haven't seen
much weather yet

Like a hard drizzle
you're still happy to be in
The kind that makes people dance
and kiss
and propose

Some people have clouds in their eyes
or their rain is over the ocean
or the Dead Sea
or it's just a sprinkle
when you needed a hurricane

Let them stay young
and always ready for sun.

      For Madeline,
      You deserve a weightless world

Searching For Daughters

The dust turned to plaster
after so much moisture.
The door isn't old
but this part of town doesn't see
a lot of sun.
Leaving everything wet.
Still dripping from yesterday's fog.
The inside was no reprieve.
It was humid
and my lungs were damp.
Lots of bodies crowded around
a stage
and somebody's daughter.
So many souls drowning in here,
and here I am
in the corner
coming to drown myself too.

It's only whiskey and beer here.
You don't need much
to kill yourself
or everything else.

I stood in the corner
and in the rat den knot
of pulled down paper boy caps
and flipped up peacoat collars
hiding square jaws
and 4 day beards
I saw my father.

He was sitting towards the back
of he front group, closest to the stage.
He had a glass
half full.
I never saw him drink it
the whole time I was there.
Once in a while,
he would hold it up to his chin

and just stare into it.
It was probably the same glass
he's had since we stopped talking
10 years ago.
The same glass he held
when he drove into someone's daughter.
Not a word since then.
And here he was
forever searching
for daughters
and here I was
searching for myself.
The outside air tasted good
once I left.

Sangria

Onomonopia
And the sounds of sangria
on the back of your tongue
when you desperately need to be a
warrior.

Howling mistress
The color of distress
and you're pushing all your pain
through a bleeding throat to impress
ghosts.

Heart sore
baring it all on a kitchen floor
emptying your ribcage contents
until there is no more
to offer

So, onomonopia
and the sounds of sangria
on the back of your tongue and your ears
when you need to be a
warrior

A Record for You

Scratch me as hard as you can
you have a need
and I will wail as loud as you want me too\
Spin me until I'm empty
until there's nothing left
to hear from me
until I just repeat the last 3 seconds
        the last 3 seconds
        the last 3 seconds
        the last 3 seconds

Flip me over
and I'll start again
just like that

I know I'm not the fanciest
and sometimes I stutter
but I will always play for you

even when I'm bending far past my limits
or revealing the small cracks of a bigger problems
and when you lay me down right on my side
when I want to stand up next to you

Caged Family

Family is just a cage
that you love to hate to live in.
But when you're gone,
you hate to love missing it.

So Much More

I signed up to be a father last night
Agreeing to marry a mother.
More commitment than I'm used to.
And we were entangled in each other
's lives.
None of us know quite what we're doing.
We talked about fears.
My biggest one being like my dad.
"That's all of our biggest fear," she said.
"You're all I've ever wanted."
I'm glad we finally met each other.
I just want to be good to you.
You deserve so much more than you've been given.

My Father's Blood

What does it mean to have my father's blood in me?
Thump thump pumping
into the smallest cells in my body.
A small reservoir
every atom marinates in.
But it's all dog's blood.
Making me want to hit women
and break things.
Like my boy's arm
on his 12th birthday
for not blowing out all the candles
and embarrassing me.
Blood that clots up behind my eyes
so I can never cry.
There is a sparrow with a candle
in my ribbed cage.
But all this blood eclipses the light.
It pools in my shoulders
to weigh me down.
And the backs of my knees
so I can't stand up
for myself.
What does it mean
to have my father's blood?
Infected and rotten.
Bits of black inside red.
I want to be a good man,
but it's hard with
my father's blood.

Travis

"When can I bend you over the table?"
He asks
to my girlfriend.

"I have a boyfriend"
She mumbles
into the buttons of his shirt.
"We all have someone waiting
for us to come home."

Fingers hooking belt loops
to pull them closer
or drive couples apart.
A sweaty palm up the front of her shirt.
My shirt.

We were running late one day,
and she couldn't find her own.
Now, it was her favorite
and it smelled like him.

"We need to stop"
She whispers into his shoulder
holding the front of his pants.

"I need to be home by 6"
She breathes.

"I can do that"

The first button causality.

A Blanket

There is pain between us
and it takes up about 2.5 feet.
It doesn't breathe
or move
but it sits between us
& stops us from talking.
It's heavy
and suffocates us.
The only thing we can manage
is to look at the other person's hands
sitting alone
waiting for the space to close
so we can stop being alone
under the same blanket.

A Mom a Knife.

I was six when I first heard a *911* call.
I was lying in bed, listening
to the monsters fighting down the hall.
The things they usually fought about.
Things only monsters would understand.

Tonight was different though.
It was a new type of Hell.
The ritualistic cycle of yelling
and steady sounds of shards of broken cups
spraying outwards from the kitchen
were replaced with something else.
Something scarier.

The sound of my father's voice cracking.
Pleading to the phone to send help.
        SHE'S OUTSIDE RIGHT NOW
I got out of my bed and looked down the hallway.
The feets of my Ninja Turtles onesie
made small sparks on the carpet
in the dark.
Small purple kisses.
      YOU NEED TO SEND SOMEONE

He was standing with one hand against the wall
supporting his weight
and everyone's, apparently.

A *thud* from downstairs.

    SHE'S TRYING TO GET INSIDE

I stood in the dark,
only illuminated by a nightlight
of two penguins rocking their baby.
Irony is not lost on me.

Thud. Smash. Crack.

YOU NEED TO SEND SOMEONE NOW. HELP US!

The downstairs monster was screaming.
Nothing human.
Nothing a person could understand.
Just various tongues of anger.

The final *crack* and my father spun to find my eyes.
The door had surrendered.

SHE'S INSIDE
I watched as the phone dropped at the same time
he reached out to close my door.

I'M GONNA TO KILL HIM

Just before the door shut,
he whispered
                stay here. don't come out no matter what you hear.
I nodded.

I'M GONNA FUCKING KILL HIM

The sound of her feet coming up the stairs.

I used this time to build a small cube
of blocks
to put my bear in.
If nothing else,
the bear would be safe.

I grabbed a light blue Swiss Army knife.
A single blade
I had found in my dad's drawer.

I didn't know anything about it
other than that
I could use this
to keep my bear safe.

Stop it, please

GET OUT OF MY FUCKING WAY

This was not a normal night.
No yelling.
No crashing dishes.
Nothing to clean tomorrow before school.
Just the sound of muffled thuds
in front of my door.
And the *snaps* of my door being pushed into its frame
from the outside

       PUT IT DOWN
           I'M GONNA STAB HIS FUCKING HEART OUT
       STOP IT

I just stared at the door,
dancing in its frame.
Creaking and moaning and snapping
and begging to let them both fall into me.
Just a strip of light
broadcasting their feet
locked in a battle.

The door handle jiggled
and I stood in front of my bear bunker.
Knife raised and ready.

The door momentarily opened
and I stopped breathing.
This was the moment I was going to die.
I was sure of it.
The monster had killed my father
and was going to stab me
just like she had promised.
The door opened two inches
before being slammed shut.

The sound of feet running across the house.
Slamming the bathroom door in their bedroom.
The sound of hysterical crying.
The sound of my father's work shirt
scratchy and dirty

sliding down the front of my bedroom door
until he hit carpet.
The sound of breathing.
The sound of sirens in the distance.
No one came to comfort me that night.
Or to check on the bear.

Marko

I'm sick of dating your ex
Every word he said
came through my mouth
like his fingers on your arm
were mine.
Like "whore" and "cunt"
and "you'll never find someone better than me"
filled the slits between my teeth, and crawled in your veins
Like all his late work nights
were my coworkers
and friends.
I can't keep dating your ex
My shoes are not his
not is my chest
or this poe,
or my words

I feel like I know his skin
has the same texture
as the eggshells I walk on
and I must know him so well.
The words he said
the way he laughed
how he walked
and never wanted to
slide his hand down
to yours
so now I can't either.
I know it all
like it's my own
more than I know you
I know who he is.

When I picked you up at the airport
I carried your dufflebags and backpacksduffle bags
full of shredded paper.
It's taken a long time to piece them together
only to see that they just repeat
        MARKO

over and over and over
until the weight
kills us both.
I'm not dating you
if I'm always dating your ex.
If we're always dating your ex

The day I came to surprise you at work
you and him were in the back room
leaning against the freezer
and sitting on a box of mangoes.
Clearly, great minds think alike
but so do hopeless ones
since he and I both wanted time.

When we get home later
on the couch
or the bed
you'll be distracted by him.
I'm not your ex
but at time,
I wish I was.
Because that when you're most present.

Be Naked

A kid asked me what they should be when they're my age
so that by the time they're dust
they're dust that did it right.
Be naked, kid.
Be naked to the world
but keep your clothes on
except when someone allows you to remove them.
Be naked to everyone.
You can't hide anything when you're naked,
so be that to every person you meet.
Open.
Honest.
Vulnerable.
So vulnerable that it hurts sometimes.
That you bleed through your tissue skin
Keep it thin
& naked.
So when someone asks what's wrong,
you can tell them.
And you'll never know what it's like
when your chest is tight
and you neck feels stiff
from carrying so much.
But, if you do, you'll know what it's from.
Be naked and honest to the world.
To those you love
To those you don't
Just be open & raw.
Not afraid to show your ugly parts
because nothing is ugly if we all share it.

Finishing

You said you had a headache
I asked if you could still eat peanut butter
You went pee four times in two and a half hours
I asked if that was normal
when you threw up the next morning
we both stared at your stomach in silence
wondering what our lives would be like
this time next year
I never said a word though
neither did you
We could have handled this better
but we're both lost
and all of this is too new for us
It makes us feel like children
or, more accurately,
helpless adults
not able to control the things children know
nothing about
There is an innocence in the loss of innocence
Our typical Saturday night tradition of burying
a bottle of cheap wine in our guts
and giggling as we take advantage of each other
was replaced with a bottle of orange juice
and a movie neither of us watched
There were no words to make this better
We didn't make much sound that weekend;
just socked souls on carpeted floors
The brilliant dance of acting like nothing changed
choreographing ourselves away from one another
saying only what was needed
to keep life going
as usual
until I whispered the first half of
"I'm sorry"
into her ear Sunday night
not being able to finish the sentence
leaving both of us wondering if we could ever
finish what we start.

Pearl Necklace

In 1949, Marybeth Loon inherited her mother's pearl necklace.
The one her father gave her.
She wore it every day,
always remembering how much it meant to her mother.
When she died, it sat in her son's bedroom.
Until it was stolen.
And sold to a pawn shop.

A little girl bought it, and kept it for many years.
Eventually giving it to her lover
before he went on his missionary journey.
He kept it in his pocket for two years
before giving to an inmate in a prison.

The day the man was sentenced to die,
he wrapped the pearls around his knuckles.
The firing squad raised their guns
and he clenched his pearls.
You are those pearls.

The most beautiful thing
that can be clenched
in difficult times.

Causing knuckles to become the color of clouds
as the greys and the pinks and the whites all blend together.

You are the moment people hold onto
when they have nothing else.

And despite everything
you will make a life better.

Oxygen Mask Abridged

You keep the glass of scotch close to you mouth,
covering your nose
like an oxygen mask.

I always wondered what would happen if I saw you without it.

Oxygen Mask

Most of my childhood, I saw you with an oxygen mask.
Carrying it around the house,
sometimes pulling it away from your face to speak,
sometimes you just whispered into the bottom of the mask
letting your words float
in a vacuum
always hoping they might escape.
They swam.

You carried that mask with you to dinners
and trips to the park
on airplanes
and fourth grade choir concerts.

I never saw you refill it
nor did I see you drink from it.
Just breathing
like a hurt kid who knows they're not supposed to leave their room
so they just rub their fingers on bottom corners of the door.

The day I graduated college
I saw your mouth
for the first time
as you put the glass down to say
I'm proud of you.

We all breathed air for the first time that day.

Hard Things To Hear

A group of us sits in a circle
with our eyes closed
whispering the thing we needed to hear
as a child
into each other's ears

None of this was your fault

I love you

You're a good kid

Things will be ok.

Dirty Christ on a Brown Mule

Christ, you speak like God
In tongues I don't understand
I've tried for years to decide
your scripture and commandments
but I find myself on the tips of mountains
shouting at clouds
with a sacrificial son
and an observant sun
(or the other way around)
just to try and understand your mutterings.

Like Me, Like You, Like a Baptismal Pool

Christ,
I was just about killed when you asked
how you can grow up like me.
Kid,
just wait a few years.
You just don't know it yet.
At your age,
bright eyed & bushy tailed,
adults have it all together.
Never floundering.
Always knowing what to do.
But we're all just
one poorly timed breath
away from inhaling water
and sulfur.
Saying you want to be me
is a baby drowning in a baptismal pool
Sad as Hell
but you can't lose the irony
of good intentions
because, kid, I never wanted you to be like me.
I wanted you to be better.

Typical Schedule

60 hr's a week
plus school
Full time
I don't get enough sleep
but I can function
Well
Really well
I seem happy
but I can't stop thinking about dying
Homework, homework, work, home, home, work
A date a few times a week
eat a couple days, when I have time
But underneath the thinest layers of my eyes
is a vision of me hanging in a bathroom
Look for apartments
Write a poem
Hope it helps
Pizza, date night, don't cry
Normal week

Death March

I'm on a death march
legs drag
eyes swell.
I just can't stop.
March on, boy. March on.
Straight from a breakup
to unemployment
to homelessness
to the things people deal with normally
but I just can't.
Not all the same week.
It's not a jog
with a bump in the road.
It's a death march
with a missing body.
Out at sea,
with $10,000 in cash
withdrawn from a bank account
hoping a faked death
won't tip off the life insurance
that will pay for sister's college.
Only to end up dead anyways
because who really wants to run away.
What we really want when we say we want to run
is *hold me, and tell me I'm safe here.*
I am not safe.

Please, tell me sister I am sorry.
And do not tell anyone about the $10,000 under her bed.
We don't want to spoil the life insurance.
You are the culmination of millions of years
of stardust,
all vying to create.
Millions of years of dust
wanted nothing more than to become you
and it did
and it is so beautiful.
Don't forget we're just dust.
Do your best

but it's ok if we fail.

And to my dad,
you were always the one.
The one who struggled
and made me laugh
and screamed
and loved
and were human.
It's ok to be human.
You always were one.

Mom,
you are good.
So good.
You are the shoes that wrap these feet
when they blister,
and the jacket
that beats away the cold
with a frying pan
and a block of cheese.
Stay good.
I know it's hard.

Be kind.
And vulnerable.
And scared.
And loving.

It's all just a death march anyways.
You can only do it smiling.

Gods' Cemetery

When bodies die,
their souls go to Heaven
or Hell.

But where do souls go
when they die?

Another place
another room
with a lake
of nothing.

Thousands of dead Gods
sitting around a table.
Or rotting in chains.

Lucifer, Hermes, Vishnu,
Jesus the Christ
They're all there.
And none of them expected
they were just as insignificant
as those they watched
for millenniums.

Now, they sit
under they eye of a higher power
which will someday die
and find itself at a table
in a room
with a lake.

The Storyteller

In third grade
my teacher sent home a note
explaining that I was a storyteller:
a disrupter
Distracting the students for my selfish narcissism
I went to school the net day
with a dark blue hammock under my eye
like a scarlet letter
to let me know who I was.
Because, in my house,
children learn best when they pool blood.

I met a boy named Dez
who told me about his own hammocks.
We spent the next 7 years
trading stories,
educating each other that
belts don't just work on pants
and vases aren't just for flowers
and stoves do so much more than cook.
All the time,
letting the other know that they weren't alone.
We were the only ones in our club,
but we understood what an absence meant
or sunglasses
or asking to hang out just a few more minutes;
just to hear more stories,
and not go home.
Because our words were our homes.

Desmond Welting hung himself at 23 years of age,
and here I am,
still telling stories.
But the teacher was wrong.
These stories were never for me.

Rain

I stood in the storm with you
for two hours.
Under an umbrella,
huddled.
It was exactly two and a half inches too low for me.
So I slouched
like a babbling baby
pretending to be a drunk God
just watching your lips destroy me.
I was soaking wet
as we stood up to our ankles
in a flood.
I was flooded.
I could smell your hair
and I was shaking underneath my jackets.
My back screamed when I stood up
like a xylophone falling down stairs.
Each bone breaking back into place.
But I was too scared to move,
worried that you would realize how late it was.
I just stood and laughed and watched your mouth
and thought about your boyfriend.

What they're doing isn't going to accomplish anything
Protest does not equal riot
        Does not equal looting
                Does not equal criminal
I don't hate blacks. I hate black culture.
Black does not equal African American
        Does not equal Urban
                Does not equal criminal
It doesn't help to separate
black and black culture.
Like a flag torn down
circled by vultures
who only hate the east-facing side.

Privilege is a pair of glasses whose tint block out the gifts you receive
so you think that all have those same presents.

132

Music

There once was a hurricane
that destroyed most of a cemetery
Leaving only a few tombstones
to remember loved ones
left standing.

When I was a boy,
I used to play a game
where I would give each tombstone a note
depending on how high out of the ground it was standing,
and I would just walk through the cemetery
singing the song of tiny stone angels
Even then, I knew the flats and the minors were too much
for young hearts.

The last time I saw my father,
he was not strong.
He was not brave
or courageous.
He was just reading.
He held the newspaper,
as he did every day,
and he just folded it in half,
ever careful to keep the crease
and then fell towards the table.
The ways the plates bounced
and left that double *clap*
is part of the song that day.
Crash, clap clap, wail, sirens, wail, shoes, wail wail, wheels on linoleum, drip
drip
breathe.
whisper
I'm sorry
collapse.

The song my sister's lungs made
was a sad jazz.
Just the steady roll of a crash cymbal
stretching out its last shake.

Not wanting to stop dancing.
Not ever.

There are little bells under the vowels on my typewriter,
so when I write,
there is always a song.
Always there.

But when I am away,
there is still a song
in the air
in the way people blink
in tombstones
and lungs
and dinner plates
and the crackle of a newspaper folding.

It is with me.
A journal
embroidered on my ear drum.
I keep collecting songs.

In my next life, please let me be deaf.

Patches of Grass

It seems unfair
to have so much grass dead
just to dig a hole.

Unfair like how devastating
the clouds are
when you see familiar shapes.
Unfair like how the world continues
unfazed
uncaring
unaltered
And you wish strangers like the barista
were in the hole with them.

You just want them to shake
like the ground
Shake like the trees,
like the boy in the cold
Shake like you,
Like me.

Unfair that your entire world collapsed
Yet everyone else's get to continue on.
A man woke up this morning
to dig a hole.
Someone made $3.45 off your shoe polish
so you can see the capillaries
of your social network
in the dirt
while your tendons tighten,
curled into row boats
to carry you away,
but everywhere you go,
people don't know about all your dead grass.

Quixote

You keep whispering to yourself
that you can save the world.
Save the people.
Save yourself.
What a fool,
what a hero
to think you can save anything.

Like giants on windmills,
there are nothing to be saved
that can be.

Like Quixote,
you charge forward.

Like a fool.
Mad reckless
charge rumbling through a field on fire
with your weight in water
to wet the tongues of sufferers.

How romantic the idea is
that you can pull someone from churning waters
where they have thrown themselves against the rocks
for years.
How foolish to think you can lift them up
out of the water,
dry them off,
and help them swim again.

It's crazy.
Crazy like Quixote.
Crazy like you.
Crazy like what I want to believe in.
How mad you must be to believe
in something
that seems impossible.
Like tying strings to the feathers of birds
so the whole sky becomes a net

to catch the sun in.
Not to keep,
but to share with the people
who never see it.
How I wish I was so mad.

Nicole

The way you spun your coffee
in a small hurricane
made me dizzy.
Either that,
or the ring in your eyes.
A ring I would wrap you in
if I could.
I'm so dizzy though.
From your coffee
and your smile
and your teeth
and the exasperated look on your face
when you can't think of an adjective
to describe the noun
you're presently verbing about.

The corners of your mouth danced that day.
Little flickers with tap shoes
Playing music
in the rings of my eyes.
Rings I would wrap yours in
like blankets
built for two.
But I'm dizzy.
Dizzy from hearing about how you're in love
with your ex.
He jumped out of planes
into the ocean
to save lives.
How could I ever compete with that.

Sometimes I dip my pen in ink,
and proceed to stain my fingertips.
That is adventure for me.
And this.
The coffee.
And you.
And your words.
And your rings.

Woke up

When I asked you what your thoughts were
on the remainder of the poem,
you just told me to
trim it down.
To cut out
the unnecessary parts.

Parts like "I woke up"
because it's assumed
you woke up,
after all.

But I kept it in there
because it's still important
On days where I fall asleep
praying to God
that it can just end with me falling asleep
I wake up.

Dear God,
I think you misunderstood me
because I woke up.

Dear God,
I think I misspoke
because I woke up.

Dear God,
Are you even there?
Because I woke up.
Despite my objections to doing so.

So,
while you consider it something
pretty well understood,
I consider it a miracle.

Permission

After a long day
I managed to make it home
close the door behind me
and that's about it.

My knees are the first things to collapse
onto the floor.
Then my hands.
Then I just sort of crumpled over.

I didn't say a word.
I just cried.
Pieces of me fell to the ground
and exploded
like grenades.
Like how Hemingway fished.
Sticks of TNT to blow the guts out of baby minnows
Because some things are overkill and dramatic.
but not this.
Not me
right now.

The bones jut out of my chest
like a piano
begging me to play them.
You whisper,
You don't have to break off pieces of yourself
to create music.

I was told to just get over it.
but some days are just too much for me.
Like Anne Sexton.
I was told to write more poetry
to feel better.

I have been told to feel better so many times,
I could crumple those statements up into rocks.
The rocks inside the pockets of Virginia Woolf.

I just shake
like a baby drowning in a baptismal pool.
Born again and dying in the same breath.
Like Sylvia Plath.

You whisper,
Bend yourself backwards
against the current.
The water is dark & burns cold.
You have seen people die here
when they cast themselves against rocks
over & over
too proud, too scared
to grab hands of those on shore
waiting to take them in
& warm them.

Your whispers keep me from
Cobain
or Thompson
or Wallace
or Brautigan
or maybe I need better heroes.

Or permission to take myself in.

They Looked Like Creation

They looked like creation.
Like art
or poetry
or dance.
Standing, leaning against a wall
hoping that someone will think they're good enough
to take home.

They stood like a painting,
with strong lines in Crayon
knowing a lot of people won't accept their child spark
but still hoping to be an adult.

They moved like a poem
clumsy, at times,
but begging thoughts about breathing
to be shared with someone who enjoyed
the clumsy
and the beauty.

Like a dance
you don't understand,
they just sang
and spoke to you.
You'll never know why,
because the words don't exist
except in art
and poetry
and dance
and creation.

Begging

Every time I love,
it comes about differently.
Some loves are slow
and organic,
like seeing an old friend
and hugging them tight.

Some are quick,
like a shooting star.
Fast, and bright,
and radiating
through the entire
night sky.

Sometimes, it's like a vine.
Slowly growing
and creeping
and strangling.

Some loves are like
begging a garden to grow.
Sowing and seeding
and watering
and pleading.
Pleading with the dirt
underneath your fingers
to have meaning.

Slow-motion
like a car accident
you can't get out of.
Knowing the impact will hurt,
and seeing the face of the driver coming towards you.
Eyes.
You always notice the eyes.
Right before a collision.

Sometimes, I fall in love like that.
And I come out dirty

and broken
and bruised
and brilliantly lit up
and begging
for another shot.

My Friend and I

Suicide does not have to occur in a single moment.
It can, and usually does,
stretch out over a life time.
Every moment we do
just brings us towards a cliff
rushing at our feet.

So when my friend told me she was struggling
with that look in her eye
that said
It has already taken everything I have
just to say this.
I know not to ask what's going on.

I've seen her scars.
Like bolts of lightening from her heart
running down her sleeve.
I know exactly what eyes look like
when they stop seeing hope.
I see them in her.
But I don't have the courage to ask her
What is going on?
What can I do to help?

I know her well,
so I know that the curves of her mouth
are usually upturned.
Dancing.
So, right now,
when they lay flat,
I don't have the guts
to tell her
She'll survive.
I know that surviving is the reason she feels this way.

When we were both little,
she fell and scraped her knee.
I didn't know what to do then,
so I just held her.

Tight.
Until someone came to help.
There is no one coming now.
And I'm too scared
to hug her.
I know it won't do much.
It is hard to love someone who doesn't feel worthy of it.

I know that feeling too,
but I can't bring myself to tell her.
To show her my own wounds.

When all I really want to do is tear up my sleeves,
and say
See!
You are not alone in this.
Look! Look with your eyes,
God dammit, Look!
I wish I could show her every wound
from every night
I spent up in bed
just staring at the ceiling
thinking of which tree will hang me.
I wish I could tell her the same reasons I have to keep going,
but most of my list is just her name.
and how do I communicate that?

We both feel powerless sometimes.
That's why our eyes feel faded,
our shoulders buckle,
and we walk with the weight of the world.

But never have I felt as powerless
as when a friend told me
she struggles like I do.

Wealth and Grad School

My best friend is rich
Wealthy
And I hate him for it
So we have conversations
where I challenge myself
To drink from his champagne glasses
while forgetting I didn't eat today
He is good
very good
but I remember
sneaking in the windows
of a foreclosed home
while we figure out which one
of his houses
we should play video games at
I am so happy for him
but my heart is a harbor
of many things
I've wanted to say
to His People
Not him
of course
Not him

My Son Like Me

I thought my biggest fear
was being a father
like my father
and his before him.
I thought that
the day I have a child,
I would turn into a monster
barreling through the house
chasing rag dolls.

Fear is strange,
in that it always seems to surprise you,
coming out of your weak spots.

The day my son comes home from school
and just wants to sleep,
I won't be suspicious.
I will think he had a long day,
and he is wiped out.

The time when he puts his backpack on
over dirty clothes
and tousled hair,
I probably won't think much of it.
Because boys are just little dirty sometimes.

When he breaks up with his first partner,
and he doesn't leave his room for days,
I will think it's normal.
Breakups are hard.

When his first report card comes home
failing every class.
I will be surprised, because he always seemed so smart,
but every kid struggles now and then.

When we stop talking,
I will think it's because he turned 16,
and that's what you do.

I won't know he stopped talking to everyone.

When he sends me a text
saying he's not doing well,
I will call him when it's convenient for me,
because that's what my schedule allows.

I will never know his hospital visit his freshman year in the dorms.
When he breaks up with his partner,
he leaves out the part that she couldn't shoulder his pain anymore.
He started wearing long sleeves so he isn't reminded of mistakes.
He hasn't learned to love himself yet,
which makes it damn hard for others to.
We won't talk about dying, because we're both so scared of it.
And when the towel rack in his first apartment
needs to be re-affixed to the wall,
I will never question him.
Even as I see a red necklace hiding beneath his collar.
Hiding like he does in the dark.
Hiding like we do from each other.

He'll draw pictures of the things that scare him the most,
and it'll just be him and his daughter,
and he looks like me.

I was wrong
when I thought I was scared of being like my dad.
I'm scared of having my kid be like me.

In Heaven

When we die,
do we go to Heaven
with the same body we had?
Do we have the same strengths
and the same looks
and limitations?

Is the group of girls
from my high school,
always prettier and better dressed
than others
in a VIP section of Heaven?
Red carpet and bottle service?

Will the boy down the street
with cerebral palsy
be in a wheelchair?
His mom said at his funeral
he is probably dancing in Heaven now.
It must be scary to have to learn how to dance
for the first time
in front of Jesus.
That guy can do everything
(except swim).

I wonder if Desmond
who hung himself
will still have a broken neck.
Will he talk to angels
through gasping breaths?
Will Michael have the back of his skull missing?
Instead of talking,
he just has the sound of shotgun pellets
rattling against his teeth?

Will my English professor
still have his wedding band
strangling his finger?
That's where it was when his wife

shot him dead.
It seems like a punishment to force him to keep it.

What happens to babies who die at birth?
Do they grow up?
Do they learn to talk?

When I die,
will I have my same scars?
So imperfect
in the light.
If I don't have my insecurities,
am I still me?
If not, it sounds like Heaven is just picking and choosing
the best parts of me
instead of accepting me for me.
What a Christian thing to do.

The Astronomer and the Flower Girl

"You are the moon
and all of the stars
to me,"
said the astronomer
to the flower girl.
"Why, then, do you
not spend your days
looking through telescopes?"

"The dust, my dear,
in the cosmos;
we are made from
all of the same bits.
I do not need a telescope
when I can see entire
galaxies holding
a sunflower."

"You big-eyed man,
you just look for adventure.
You see worlds in front of you,
and move like a comet.
Coming into my orbit
and exploding.
If there are pieces left
of you,
I will take them,
and water them,
and help you grow.
Are you content
though,
being the astronomer
instead of the astronaut?"

The man held his breath.
Silent like a satellite.
"There are rivers
and seeds
and mountains

and trees,
and so much to explore
with you."

Am I good enough now, dad?

I am.

And thank you for helping me see that.

ABOUT THE AUTHOR

Writing about myself for the sake of writing about myself has always seemed a bit self-masturbatory. I've spent my life writing so that I could attempt to cope. It's the same reason any writer writes, despite whether they say otherwise. My writing has been an integral part of my identity development; and through the process of writing, I'm constantly learning new things about myself. Thank you for reading. Here's to our well-being.

-Jude

Made in the USA
San Bernardino, CA
06 May 2017